GREATEST FOOTBALL STARS

ACCESS THE ACTION!

Scan the QR code to
hear this story for
FREE!

Published in the UK by Sweet Cherry Publishing Limited, 2025
Unit 4u18, The Book Brothers Business Park, Tolwell Road,
Leicester LE4 1BR, United Kingdom

Sweet Cherry Publishing Limited
Unit 31, The Pottery, Bakers Point,
Pottery Road, Dún Laoghaire,
Dublin A96 EV18, Ireland

2 4 6 8 10 9 7 5 3

ISBN: 978-1-80263-539-3

Greatest Football Stars:
George Best

Text by Luke Paton
Illustrations by Sophie Jones

www.sweetcherrypublishing.com

Printed and bound in Turkey

MIX
Paper | Supporting responsible forestry
FSC® C111584
FSC www.fsc.org

Sweet Cherry

GEORGE BEST

THE UNOFFICIAL STORY

WRITTEN BY
LUKE PATON

CONTENTS

1

BEST OF THE BEST

On the 9th of March 1966, Manchester United were set to play against Benfica in the quarter-final of the European Cup (now called the UEFA Champions League). It was the second leg, and the match was taking place at the Estádio da Luz in Lisbon, Portugal.

Nineteen-year-old George Best heard the deafening noise of the stadium before he saw the pitch. It was so loud it made the hairs on the back of his neck stand up.

I'm ready, he thought. *This is the sort of stage I am meant to play on.*

Even though Manchester United had won the first leg 3-2, they were not the favourites to win this second match. Benfica had never been beaten in a European Cup game at their home stadium, and they'd already won the trophy twice before in 1961 *and* 1962. Benfica also had a star player on their team – Eusébio.

Eusébio had won the 1965 European Footballer of the Year award (now called the Ballon d'Or), and he was fast becoming one of the greats of the game.

But George wasn't scared. He didn't feel threatened by the thousands of fans cheering for the opposite team, or by Benfica's star players. George knew that this was *his* time to shine!

The Manchester United manager, Matt Busby, told his team to keep things tight for the first half. He knew it was going to be a close game, and he didn't want to throw away their lead early on.

It was a sensible plan. If the team managed to keep a clean sheet, they'd go through to the semi-final. The only way to do that was to defend well.

George did what Busby asked ... for the first six minutes.

Then Bobby Charlton won a free kick. Tony Dunne delivered the ball towards Benfica's box where George was standing. He had two defenders crowding around him, and he felt the goalkeeper jumping towards him too.

But George still managed to leap for the ball and get to it first.

I've made good contact, George thought as the ball shot towards the goal.

George sprawled on the floor and twisted to see what was happening. He was just in time to see the ball fly into the back of the net!

Goal! Manchester United was 0-1 up, and the game had barely even started!

We're now in with a real chance of winning! George thought.

Another six minutes passed.

George got the ball on the halfway line. He remembered Busby telling them to keep things tight. Maybe he should pass it to one of his teammates instead of going for goal?

But George didn't want to play negative football.

He feinted and ducked around a defender. Another defender approached, but George was faster than him. All of a sudden, it was just him against the goalkeeper.

The goalie came out to close him down. Which way was he going to go?

Left or right? It didn't matter! George blasted the ball past the keeper before he even knew what was happening.

George had scored two amazing goals in thirteen minutes! Against all odds, it was now 0-2 to Manchester United.

His inspired play lifted the entire team, and they were 0-3 up by half-time. In the second half, Manchester United were so determined to score that they even scored an own goal for Benfica! Incredibly, the match ended at 1-5.

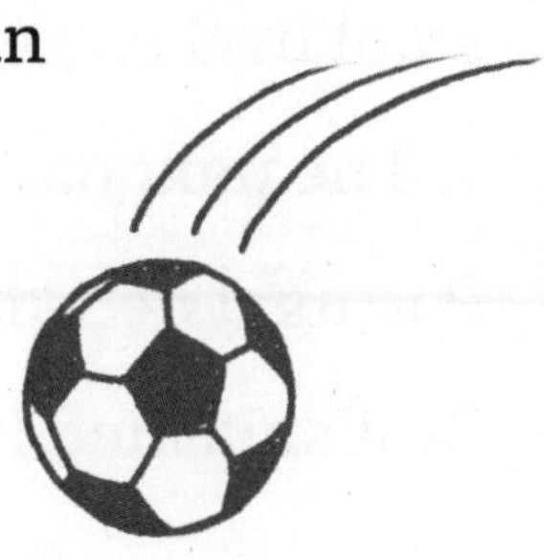

Thanks to George's determination to push forward, Manchester United were one step closer to making their dream of winning the European Cup a reality.

The manager wasn't even annoyed that George hadn't listened to his instructions. 'Our plan was to be cautious,' he said, 'but thankfully somebody must have stuffed cotton wool in George's ears.'

The next day, a newspaper in Portugal declared, 'A Beatle called Best smashed Benfica'. The nickname stuck. George was the 'fifth Beatle' because he looked just like one of the members of the incredibly popular band The Beatles!

George was the most famous man in England when the team returned home to Manchester. He wore a massive sombrero to greet photographers off the plane, and the image of him in his oversized hat was seen all around the world. Everyone wanted to either be him or be his friend.

Although George was still only nineteen years old, he'd been playing professional football for two years by that point. And now he had the world at his feet. He couldn't believe how much he had achieved since first kicking a ball in his home in Northern Ireland.

2

HOMEGROWN HERO

George Best was born on the 22nd of May 1946 in Belfast, Northern Ireland.

His father, Dickie, worked in the shipyards as an iron-turner, and he worried about his children finding stable jobs when they grew up. Lots of people in the area where George grew up struggled to find work. That's why Dickie insisted that George studied to be a printer. It was a 'proper job' that would set him up for life.

George did as his father asked, but he didn't want to be a printer. Even though he knew it was unrealistic, he wanted to be a professional footballer instead. He'd been kicking a ball around ever since he could walk. His passion for the game shone through in every match he played – no matter how big or small.

After school, George and his friends played football all afternoon and evening until it was time to go to bed. Even when it got dark, their games carried on under the streetlights.

George's favourite day of the week was Saturday. That's when he got to catch the local bus to a football pitch, strap on his boots and play a real match!

His favourite team as a young boy was the Wolverhampton Wanderers, and he loved watching them play on TV. George's family didn't actually have a TV, but he still found a way to watch every game.

Before each Wolves game started, George kicked a football against his neighbour's wall. He knew that Mr Harrison (his neighbour) always watched the matches on his TV. He also knew that Mr Harrison would eventually come out and ask, 'Do you fancy coming in and watching the game with me?' George was in there before Mr Harrison could even finish asking the question!

However, George's obsession with football did cause some problems for the Best family. When he was old enough, George started going to a grammar school that was known for playing rugby. George tried to play rugby, but it just wasn't for him. He only wanted to play football, so he started skipping school.

George didn't want his mother to know that he wasn't going to school, so he came up with a plan. On his way home, he bought sweets that turned his tongue red if he sucked them hard enough.

After telling his mother, Anne, that he'd been sent home with a sore throat, he'd show her his bright red tongue as proof.

Unfortunately for George, he tried this trick once too often. Anne believed him at first, but she soon became very worried and took him to the doctor. This led to George having an operation to remove his tonsils! He had to go along with it, or else his mother would know he was lying.

When George's parents realised that he was unhappy at school, they switched him to a secondary school with a football team.

The first side George played for was Cregagh Boys. He was thirteen years old and already showing massive talent. The coach, Bud McFarlane, thought he was too slim and too shy to go professional. But McFarlane also thought George had all the makings of a star player. There was certainly nobody else who trained as hard as George.

One day, McFarlane told George that he relied on his right foot too much. To correct this, George spent the next week in training using only his left foot. When the team played a match at the weekend, George didn't even wear his

right football boot! He just used his left foot for the whole game and somehow scored twelve goals!

Despite this incredible showboating, George couldn't get any bigger clubs to take a chance on him. A scout from Glentoran thought he was 'too wee' to make it in professional football. Another scout from Leeds United agreed that George was too skinny to compete with stronger players.

But McFarlane knew a star when he saw one. He convinced Bob Bishop, the top scout in Northern Ireland for Manchester United, to take a look at George.

The first time Bishop saw George was in a match between Cregagh Boys and Boyland FC. At first, Bishop did *not* like what he saw. Like the other scouts before him, he thought George was too small to make it as a professional.

But then he saw George play ...

After the final whistle, Bishop was in no doubt about George's skills with a football. George was much better than anybody else on the pitch, and he was never muscled off the ball by the bigger players. While most of the Boyland team were seventeen or eighteen years old, George was still only fifteen!

Bishop later sent a telegram to the manager of Manchester United, Matt Busby. The telegram was made up of only eight words, but they were words that changed George's life forever. It read: *I think I have found you a genius.*

3

MADE IN MANCHESTER

In July 1961, fifteen-year-old George and his friend Eric McMordie made their way to Manchester from Belfast. The two boys had never left their home before, and here they were crossing the Irish Sea on a ferry! It was a scary feeling to be striking out on their own

– and everything seemed to go wrong for them at first.

When the boys got to Manchester, they asked a taxi driver to take them to Old Trafford.

'Which Old Trafford?' the taxi driver asked.

George had no idea Old Trafford was a cricket ground as well as a football stadium!

They made it to the right place eventually and had a tour of the training ground where Manchester United's first team (nicknamed the Red Devils) practised. George got to meet some of the star players in the current squad, including Harry Gregg and Jimmy Nicholson.

George also met the mythical Manchester United manager, Matt Busby. Busby's reputation in football was so large that George couldn't believe he was shaking hands with a genuine football legend.

It's like being introduced to God! he thought.

Busby smiled. 'So you're the boy I've heard so much about,' he said. 'Good luck to you, son.'

After that, George and McMordie went to the house where they'd be staying. It belonged to Mrs Fullaway, who had lots of experience looking after potential Manchester United players. But just like the scouts, Mrs Fullaway didn't have the best first impression of George.

Well, he'll never make a footballer! she thought.

George and McMordie took a walk around Manchester that night. It was very different from their home in Belfast, but they didn't find that exciting. They found it scary.

I feel like I don't belong, thought George.

There was something else bothering George as well.

I'm here, he thought. *Manchester United have got four teams: first team, reserves, A and B team. Plus the Youth Team. By the time I wait for all the ones in front of me to make it, it's gonna be too late.*

McMordie must have been thinking the same thing.

'I don't think I fancy this, do you?' said McMordie. 'You wanna go home?'

'Yeah, we're wasting our time,' George agreed.

The next morning, the two boys told Manchester United that they wanted to go home. They were on the ferry back to Belfast before they knew it.

George's father, Dickie, hit the roof when George came home. 'You've thrown away a chance of a lifetime!' he screamed. 'What are you doing back? What's happened? What did you do?'

'Nothing, Dad,' George replied. 'We just didn't like it there.'

'What do you mean you didn't like it? You've only been gone a day!'

Anne was a bit more understanding. 'Never mind, son,' she said, putting an arm around George.

Dickie got on the phone to Manchester United to see if anything could be done. He spoke to Joe Armstrong, who was in charge of the young players coming through.

'They're not the first to run off and they won't be the last,' Armstrong told George's father. 'It's quite normal for lads to get a bit homesick. It can be a bit daunting when they leave home for the first time. But your son is welcome back any time, Mr Best.'

George was relieved. He'd started to feel a bit silly about running away so quickly.

Two weeks later, he took the ferry back to Manchester and resettled in Mrs Fullaway's house. He was still homesick and couldn't get used to Manchester, but he didn't run back to Belfast this time.

One way or the other, he thought. *I'm going to stick it out.*

Determined to improve, George began training with Manchester United twice a week.

Bobby Charlton, one of the club's stars, soon heard about George.

'Bobby, there's a really good young lad, a great young player in the juniors, he's just coming through, a little lad from Belfast,' the coaches told him.

Well, they're laying it on a bit thick, Charlton thought. *Nobody can be as good as that*.

Then Charlton saw George train in a match against right-back John Angus. He made Angus look like a fool! From that moment on, Charlton marked George as one to watch.

Busby was also keeping a close eye on George. 'Don't tinker with the boy's style,' he told his coaches. 'Let him develop his own way, naturally. He's something special.'

George tried harder than everyone else on the training field, often staying behind to work on his skills. He loved trying to hit the crossbar from the eighteen-yard line, and his main focus was making his left foot stronger.

When he wasn't training, George worked as a clerk at the Manchester Ship Canal Company. George didn't like the job (he was mostly making cups of tea!), but it kept him busy. So long as he was working or playing, he didn't think about how much he missed his home in Belfast.

The rest of the time, George did whatever he wanted. Manchester United didn't watch him closely, but they did have one rule: all trainees had to be home before 10:30 p.m.

But George never did like following instructions. Whenever he wanted to stay out later, he'd simply escape out of the window and climb down a ladder used by the window cleaner next door. He got back in the same way, too!

Mrs Fullaway eventually rumbled his escape routine, but she didn't stop him from having a good time. Instead, she gave him a key to the front door – without telling anybody at Manchester United, of course!

The club never suspected what George was doing, mostly because he didn't let anything get in the way of his football.

Manchester United was impressed with his performances on the training pitch and with the reserve teams.

On the 22nd of May 1963, George's seventeenth birthday, he officially signed for the club. George knew that his debut for Manchester United's first team would soon follow, and he couldn't wait.

Manchester United played in the First Division (the same level as the Premier League today), so it would be a big change from playing for the reserve teams. But George felt more than ready. He was finally a professional footballer, and he intended to show the world exactly what he could do!

4

LUCKY NUMBER 7

In September 1963, George's coaches told him that he'd be making his First Division debut at Old Trafford. Most seventeen-year-olds might be nervous about playing their first game in front of 50,000 fans, but not George. He couldn't wait to get out on the field.

Before the game, he read the match programme and drank a cup of tea. He might as well have been waiting to catch a bus!

But George didn't really have to worry about disappointing any of those 50,000 fans. If anyone mentioned him in the stands before the game, they likely just said, 'George who?' Nobody outside of the club had heard of him before.

Manchester United's opponents for the match were West Bromwich Albion, which didn't faze George. The only thing that bothered him was his teammates' warnings about West Brom defender Graham Williams.

'Watch out for him, George,' they said. 'He carries a club in either foot!'

They meant that Williams was as tough as nails and likely to pummel George with hard tackles at any given opportunity. George's teammates told him to be careful, or else he might end up with a broken leg!

But when George spotted Williams on the pitch, he thought he looked kind of small.

Georgie boy, you've got nothing to worry about, he thought.

Wearing the number 7 shirt, George jogged out onto the pitch before kick-off. The roar from the crowd gave him a deep thrill and made the hairs on the back of his neck tingle.

I feel like a gladiator coming into the arena, he thought.

George lined up and waited for the referee to blow his whistle.

Minutes into the game, Williams 'welcomed' George to the First Division by clattering him with a brutal challenge.

Ouch!

It was a warning shot designed to unnerve the seventeen-year-old upstart. Williams was telling George that he wasn't about to be embarrassed by a teenager.

But George didn't take the bait. He simply shook the challenge off and got on with the game. He dribbled and ran with the ball just as he had done in training. He even managed to nutmeg Williams at one point!

His best moment came after he showed a bit of skill, gathering the ball inside his own penalty area before slipping past a challenge.

As George looked up for one of his teammates, he spotted Denis Law on the halfway line and picked him out with a perfect pinpoint pass. The crowd erupted into applause!

The manager, Matt Busby, was delighted to see that George hadn't folded under the pressure of the big game. However, he *was* concerned that Williams was giving George bruises all over his legs. In the second half, Busby switched George to the other side of the pitch.

George continued to perform well under pressure. He even played a part in Manchester United's only goal of the game, which was enough to win 1-0.

'Well done,' one of his teammates said after the final whistle.

'Good lad,' somebody else congratulated him.

'You did fine, son,' said Busby.

George celebrated by having eggs and chips for tea at Mrs Fullaway's house. He also wrote a letter to his parents boasting about the 'fabulous experience' he'd had.

But the best praise came from Busby. 'We've got an Irish boy here called Best, and if he doesn't make a genius I haven't seen one,' he said after the match. 'It's all there: the heart, the ability. Everything.'

George hoped to play for the first team more often, but he wasn't picked again for a while. He went back to playing for the reserve team.

In December 1963, George finally got another chance to play for the first team.

While he was spending Christmas with his family in Northern Ireland, a telegram came through for him. It asked him to get back to Old Trafford as soon as possible.

George thought they just wanted him to play for the reserves, but his father was convinced he was going to play in the first team ... And he was right!

George got straight on the phone. 'Look, if I come and play,' he told the coaches, 'I wanna be back in Belfast the same night and finish my Christmas with the family.'

The club agreed.

And so, George's second game for

the Red Devils was against Burnley. George was the star of the show this time. He got the better of defender Alex Elder, and he even scored his first goal for the first team.

Manchester United held up their end of the bargain, too. George was back in Belfast only hours after the Burnley game finished. He was thrilled when he read his name in a Belfast newspaper the next day!

After the game against Burnley, Busby had no choice but to keep George in the team from then on.

He played twenty-four of Manchester United's remaining twenty-six games that season, helping them finish second in the First Division. While this was a disappointing end for United, it was a season of amazing firsts for George.

George played with Manchester United legends Charlton and Law for the first time on the 18th of January 1964. The three of them formed a deadly trio, and even the best sides struggled to get past them.

A few months later, George was called up to Northern Ireland's first team. His national team debut came on the 15th of April 1964, in a 2-3 away win against Wales. Just two weeks later, he made his second appearance in a match against Uruguay – which Northern Ireland won 3-0!

After getting a taste of what it was like to play for his national team, George went back to club duty. Manchester United's under 21s side had made it to the FA Youth Cup final, and George was determined to lead the team to victory as their captain.

It was a two-legged fixture, with the first tie played at Swindon's County

Ground stadium. About 17,000 fans turned up to cheer on their teams.

Swindon took the lead halfway through the first half, but Manchester United didn't back down. They kept on pushing and creating more chances. The scoreline could have been very different, if not for the heroics of Swindon's goalkeeper Tony Hicks. He saved multiple efforts from George and the rest of his team.

Eventually, George managed to score an equaliser! He got on the end of a pass from Peter McBride and finally found a way past the keeper –

shooting the ball into the far corner! The game ended at a tense 1-1.

The second leg was played in front of about 25,000 fans in Old Trafford, and it went a lot better. Manchester United's David Sadler scored a hat-trick, and the team won 4-1.

With the total score across both legs being 5-2 to Manchester United, George claimed his first winner's medal! It was the perfect end to a frantic first season.

By then, George had played four games in less than a week: some for the first team, some for the youth team and some for Northern Ireland! Not that George minded.

'I'll play seven days a week if they let me!' he said.

Playing with iconic players in the country's biggest league was just too easy for him. It was like playing football as a kid!

People were starting to notice him, too. One newspaper called George 'truly a brilliant player heading for greatness' – and it was proved right the very next season.

5

THE FIFTH BEATLE

George was only eighteen years old when he became a regular in the Manchester United first team. It was the 1964/1965 season, and George was already getting a reputation.

On the 30th of September 1964, Manchester United met Chelsea (the league leaders) at Stamford Bridge. Law had been singled out as the Reds' main threat beforehand, but George quickly changed their minds after kick-off.

He pulled out all his magic tricks and swerves to run the Chelsea defender Ken Shellito ragged. He scored one goal and set up another for a 0-2 win. At the end of the match, George got a round of applause from both sets of fans! Shellito even rushed over to congratulate him on a game well played.

In another match against Burnley, George had some problems with his left boot towards the end of the game. But instead of sorting it out, George picked up the troublesome footwear and played the rest of the game with only one boot on. Best of all, George provided the cross for Manchester United's winning goal!

Before one match against Liverpool, he asked Paddy Crerand and goalkeeper Alex Stepney to stay behind in training.

'I want to try something,' George told them.

'What do you want?' they asked.

George set up a play that had Stepney release the ball to Crerand, who then passed the ball diagonally to George on the other wing. George waited on the halfway line so that he wasn't offside when Crerand passed to him, then he ran onto the ball.

When it came time to play the match for real, George, Crerand and Stepney executed their set piece to perfection! George scored a goal in front of the Liverpool fans and ran off laughing!

In that first full season, George scored fourteen goals in fifty-nine games for the Red Devils. His efforts helped the side top the First Division table on goal difference and win!

George was still only a teenager, and yet he'd already won the biggest trophy in the English league!

He was especially pleased that he'd had no trouble settling into a team that included iconic footballers such as Law and Charlton. These were players who he saw as heroes when he was younger. Now, the fans

were calling the three of them the 'Holy Trinity'!

The only problem George had was keeping himself entertained after training. The other members of the squad had wives and kids, so they were busy with their families, but George was a restless teenager. He usually played snooker, went to the cinema or went bowling. Anything to pass the time before he could play football again!

Eventually, word got back to Busby about George's busy personal life – and he wasn't pleased. Busby generally let George do whatever he wanted, but he did have to put his foot down sometimes.

Early in the 1965/1966 season, Busby called George into his office for a chat.

'I don't like some of the things I've been hearing about your social life,' Busby said. 'Don't start getting into the wrong company and bad habits. Keep your mind on your football and you'll be back in the side soon enough.' He also told George that he'd been left out of the team for an upcoming match.

George was shocked at first. He'd been playing well! Wasn't that all that mattered?

But it turned out to be just the thing George needed to push himself to the next level.

Not long after his talk with Busby, George gave one of his greatest performances ever against Benfica in the quarter-final of the European Cup.

It was after that match that the Portuguese press called George 'the fifth Beatle'. The Beatles were the biggest pop group in the world at the time, and George had long hair, sideburns and good looks just like the band members. And just like a pop star, George suddenly had his very own fan club.

George became the biggest star in world football almost overnight.

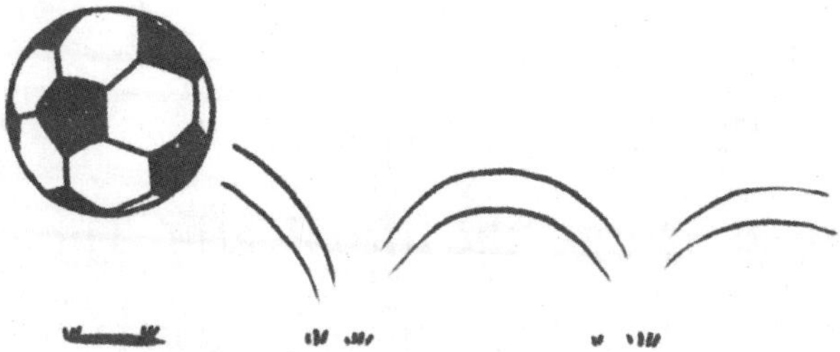

6

A STAR IS BORN

George first realised that his life had changed when he opened a clothing shop a few days after the Benfica match. Two hours before the store opened, 400 schoolgirls lined up to catch a glimpse of him!

These days, it's common for big-name footballers to appear in adverts or have their names on clothing. But it was almost unheard of in the 1960s. George was one of the first footballers to cross from the back pages of a newspaper to the front.

He also started getting fan mail – mostly from young girls who'd never watched a football game in their lives! George got as many as 5,000 letters a week. He had to employ people to take care of it for him.

He received all kinds of offers that had nothing to do with the beautiful game. People wanted him to do photoshoots or star in TV adverts. It was getting out of hand.

'George, you're going to need help with this,' Law told him. 'Why don't you use my agent?'

George accepted the offer, and soon became one of the most famous people (let alone the most famous footballer) in the country.

One of the first TV adverts George did was for Irish sausages. He asked his mother to appear in the advert with him.

'I'm not appearing in front of any TV camera!' Anne said.

But George talked her around in the end, and the whole family appeared in the advert together.

George also starred in adverts for an egg company and a clothes shop. He started making lots of money, which he spent on flashy cars for himself and his father.

But football was still George's first love, and he had a job to do for Manchester United. The Red Devils were now a force to be reckoned with in the First Division.

In the summer of 1966, England won the World Cup for the first time. Manchester United stars Bobby Charlton, Nobby Stiles and John Connelly had been part of the winning team, and they happily came back to the club with heaps of confidence.

George was glad for his teammates, but he also felt sorry for himself because Northern Ireland hadn't managed to qualify. Later in life, one of his biggest regrets was never getting to play in a World Cup.

Manchester United fans weren't worried about any of that, though.

They were just delighted that their players were full of confidence and winning games!

People especially liked watching George. 'Best baffles Leicester,' said one newspaper after his skills crushed Leicester City. 'Liverpool cannot better Best,' said another after a victory against Liverpool.

The 1966/1967 season was long and hard for Manchester United. By the time they faced West Ham in May 1967, they only needed one point to secure the league title. However, a victory against West Ham wasn't going to be easy, as they also had three World Cup-winning players in their squad.

'Let's take the game to them,' Busby said before the match. 'Each and every one of you must win your personal battle with your opposite number. Do that and the game and the Championship will be ours.'

The crowd cheered on their team as they jogged out of the tunnel. 'Champions!' they sang at kick-off.

It was all the motivation the players needed. Bobby Charlton, Bill Foulkes,

Paddy Crerand and George all scored before half-time, then Denis Law added two more goals in the second half. The match ended in an incredible 1-6 away victory.

For the second time in George's career, he'd won the First Division with the Red Devils!

In the changing room after the game, the celebrations were wild. Champagne was poured, hugs were shared and speeches were made.

'From the bottom of my heart, I would like to thank all you players,'

Busby said. 'And may I remind you that in life, there are no great men – only men.'

After their final game of the season at Old Trafford, the team got their hands on the First Division trophy. Their 60,000 fans roared as it was raised into the air.

'Our greatest aim is to win the European Cup next year,' said Busby. Everyone believed they could do it.

George was still only twenty years old at the time. It was almost unbelievable!

7

THE EUROPEAN CUP

George was in his best form for Manchester United during the 1967/1968 season. He scored twenty-eight goals in the First Division and another three in the European Cup. It was the first time he'd been the top scorer for the club in one season!

But for all of George's goals and his brilliant play, he had nothing to show for it. Manchester United lost out on another First Division title to their bitter local rivals, Manchester City. The team also got knocked out of the FA Cup in the semi-final.

It feels awful not having a winner's medal to show for all my goals, thought George.

His only chance of changing his fortunes was in the European Cup.

Manchester United eased through the first and second round, finally making it to the quarter-final. Their opponents were Polish club Górnik Zabrze – a strong side known for playing fast and purposeful football.

George was kept quiet for most of the game, after being man-marked by Górnik's Henryk Latocha. As soon as George got the chance to slip past Latocha, he took a shot that got deflected past the keeper! In the end, Manchester United won the first leg 2-0.

The conditions were insane for the second leg in Poland. The temperature was lower than zero degrees, and it was snowing when the Manchester United plane landed in Poland. A snowstorm battered against the stadium as the teams kicked off.

Manchester United couldn't manage their usual attractive football that blustery night, but they did come home having won the tie 0-1.

In the semi-final, they'd face an even tougher opponent: Real Madrid.

The first leg against Real Madrid was played at Old Trafford, and George was the only player who got on the scoresheet. This meant that

Manchester United didn't have much of a lead going into the second leg at Real Madrid's famous Santiago Bernabéu Stadium.

George's only chance of a medal looked to be danger! *This is our biggest test yet,* he thought.

120,000 fans watched the game that night in May 1968. They were treated to a magnificent display from Real Madrid in the first half, as the team used all their experience to race to a 3-1 lead. Things were looking bad for Manchester United.

During half-time, Busby gathered his team around in the changing room. 'We're only a goal down,' he said. 'And if we equalise, it could be a completely different game.'

George agreed. 'Let's have a real go at them!' he cheered.

The team talk worked. The Reds got one goal back in the 73rd minute, thanks to David Sadler.

Five minutes later, George got the ball on the wing and darted towards the touchline. He looked up and saw a red shirt in the box. He crossed, expecting to see Manchester United goalscorers Charlton or Denis get on the end of it.

To George's amazement, though, the man in the box was central defender Foulkes.

He's going to blast it wide! thought George. But Foulkes kept his head and slotted the ball neatly into the net. It was 3-3! This made the total scoreline across both legs 4-3, which meant Manchester United were going through to the final!

George rushed over to celebrate with Foulkes. 'Well done!' he said. 'But now you've done your bit, don't cross the halfway line again!'

Now only one team stood in the way of Manchester United and the European Cup. And it was an old rival: Benfica.

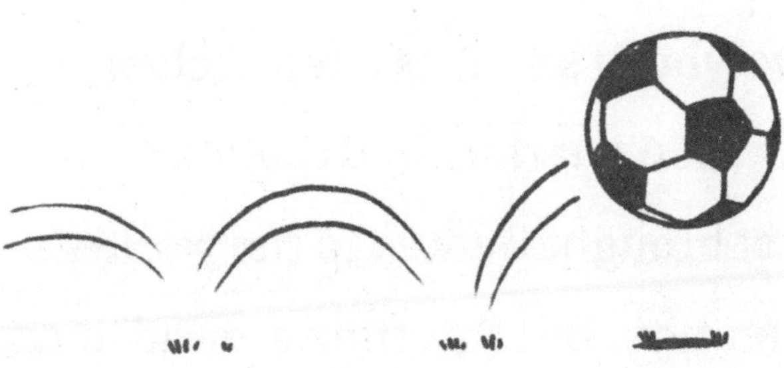

8

A FINAL TO REMEMBER

On the 29th of May 1968, Manchester United met Benfica in the European Cup final at Wembley Stadium. Everybody saw it as a rematch of the 1966 quarter-final that had first brought George to the world's attention. But this time around, it was going to be an even tougher contest.

Fans couldn't wait to watch the Manchester United and Benfica players battle it out! They would get to see Benfica's star striker Eusébio vs Manchester United's Nobby Stiles, and George vs ... well, the entire Benfica back line! Benfica didn't want a repeat of what had happened two years ago!

'I'd rather play against Eusébio than have to face George Best,' Stiles quipped before the game. 'You should see what George does to me in training. Splits me in two, he does. It gives you heart that some poor character has to try and deal with him!'

Manchester United was hoping to become the first English side to win the European Cup, so hype for the match was off the charts.

George's mother, Anne, closed the family fish and chip shop to watch the game. 'This is one game we just couldn't miss,' she said. 'It will be Manchester United by 3-1, and George will score one of them. Just you mark my words.'

The Manchester United fans hoped she'd be right. As Charlton led his team out onto the pitch, they cheered until their throats became sore.

Busby hadn't given the players much of a team talk before the match. 'Go out and enjoy yourselves, boys,' was all he said.

But Benfica was not about to let George play his usual free-flowing football. Left-back Fernando Cruz even clattered George to the ground in the opening minutes. When George tried to switch wings, he was battered by centre-back Humberto Fernandes.

By half-time, George was covered in bruises! The score was still at a very nervy 0-0.

'Let's keep playing it around, but let's get at them a bit more in the second half,' Busby told his players. 'Let's frighten them a bit more.'

George tried to pick up his team through the razzle-dazzle of his footwork. He slipped past players, flicked the ball, shot on goal and even dribbled around the referee.

The deadlock was finally broken in the 53rd minute by Charlton. His flicked header was a delight, and the fans began to believe Manchester United could actually win the cup!

But twenty-six minutes later, Benfica drew level through Jaime Graça. Once again, the atmosphere grew incredibly tense inside Wembley Stadium.

Then, in the dying minutes, Benfica had a chance to finish Manchester United off. Eusébio was straight through on goal and blasted his shot … right into the grateful hands of goalie Alex Stepney. Phew!

The final whistle blew.

It was 1-1, so the game went into extra time.

George was exhausted, and so were the rest of his teammates. They gratefully received leg rubs and water from the physios. George saw Stiles walking between the players. 'Come on, lads!' he said. 'Let's finish them off!'

'We've been giving them too much of the ball,' Busby said, 'but if we can stop doing that, we'll win this. They're getting tired, they're not used to this pitch. Let's get hold of the ball and make them do all the running.'

Three minutes into extra time, George got the ball after a long clearance from the goalkeeper. But instead of holding it up, like he was supposed to, George decided to run forward. He nutmegged an oncoming defender, skipped around the keeper … and passed the ball into an open net!

Goal! It was 2-1 to Manchester United!

Inspired by George's heroics, Manchester United didn't stop there. Two minutes later, Brian Kidd knocked in a goal, and then Charlton added a fourth in the 99th minute. It was 4-1 when the final whistle blew.

'It's all over!' the commentator screamed. 'Manchester United have done it!'

Manchester United were the European Cup winners! Charlton led the team up the Wembley steps to receive the magnificent trophy.

George swapped shirts with a Benfica player and celebrated on the pitch with all of his teammates. He'd

played the game of his life, and his team were champions of Europe.

There was more good news to come, too. At the end of 1968, George won the European Footballer of the Year award – or the Ballon d'Or, as it's called today. That meant he was officially the greatest player in Europe that year.

He was twenty-two years old and had already won two First Division titles, the European Cup and the European Footballer of the Year award. He felt on top of the world. Things surely couldn't get any better than this!

9

LAST DAYS AT MANCHESTER

After the ultimate high of winning the European Cup and the European Footballer of the Year award in 1968, George found it hard to get excited about playing football. The club didn't defend their title in 1969, and their league position slipped to eleventh.

Worse still, manager Matt Busby announced his retirement.

The rest of the team started changing, too. Top players left or retired, and George felt like the new people they brought in weren't up to his standard. The manager started to tell his team to just 'give the ball to George' and hope for the best.

I'm carrying this team! George thought.

He couldn't cope with the fans' massive expectations either. After George's devastating performances against Benfica, the supporters wanted him to perform at his best every week. When George suffered a bad day, he'd get a lot of criticism.

Eventually, the pressure got to George. He started skipping training and losing focus.

In a game against Manchester City in 1969, George got angry at the referee for giving him a yellow card. So, as the players walked off the pitch, George flipped the ball out of the referee's hands. George knew it was a silly thing to

do, but he couldn't help himself.

Unfortunately for him, the Football Association didn't see the funny side of it. They fined him £100 (almost £2,000 today) and banned him from playing for Manchester United for a month! George thought the FA were just making an example of him for being such a big celebrity.

He got even more upset when Manchester United started winning games while he was on suspension. He even got letters from people saying that the team played better without him!

But George was still capable of playing mesmerising football when he wanted to. Following his four-week suspension, he really wanted to show people what he could do.

On the 7th of February 1970, Manchester United were due to meet Northampton Town in the fifth round of the FA Cup. Northampton weren't expecting to win, but the players had been told they'd get a big bonus each if they pulled off an impossible victory. This made them very determined! Their plan to win was simple. First of all, they decided that they had to take Charlton out of the game. But their second issue was more pressing. 'If you haven't got anyone who can take care of George, you might have a bit of a problem,' they were told.

They certainly did have a problem. George had a point to prove, and he made Northampton pay for his long suspension.

This game is like an FA Cup and a European Cup final rolled into one, thought George.

George scored his first goal twenty-seven minutes after kick-off,

heading the ball into the net from Kidd's cross. His second goal came after he latched onto a through ball from Crerand. It was an extraordinary first half!

But George wasn't done yet.

In the second half, he scored a third goal and completed his hat-trick! He also added a fourth with a diving header, and then a fifth came after he connected with another pass from Crerand. But his *sixth* goal of the match was the best yet.

He shimmied past one defender in the box and then just had the keeper to beat. As soon as the keeper committed himself to one side, George went in the other direction ... and the goalie fell over! George was left to tap the ball into the goal and bask in the applause from the crowd.

Six goals in one game! It equalled the record for the most goals scored in a single game by a Manchester United player.

George's double hat-trick and two goals from Kidd meant that the match ended in an 8-2 victory!

After the game, George shook hands with the Northampton goalkeeper in the changing room. 'Don't worry about it, mate,' George said. 'There wasn't much you could do.'

'I don't really class myself as a footballer,' George boasted to the press. 'I call myself an entertainer. It's my job to do something that will send people away feeling that they'd like to see me play again.'

Unfortunately for the Manchester United fans, they were running out of time to see George light up Old Trafford in a Manchester United shirt.

10

GEORGE VS BOBBY

When George played for the Reds with Charlton and Law, the fans called them the 'Holy Trinity'. Each of these players won the European Footballer of the Year award in the 1960s – Law in 1964, Charlton in 1966 and George in 1968. They were the deadliest trio in world football! The Holy Trinity made a combined total of 1,632 appearances for the club and scored 665 goals between them. With these three men in the team, Manchester United could do anything!

But as the 1960s gave way to the 1970s, the Holy Trinity stopped firing on all cylinders. Law had an ankle injury that hobbled his later career, and Charlton wasn't as sharp as he used to be.

And George ... Well, George was just losing interest in playing football for a team past its best. More and more, his attention was drawn to things away from the pitch.

In 1970, for instance, George decided he'd had enough of staying in a house with Mrs Fullaway. He was earning a lot of money and wanted to build his dream house!

He employed an architect and gave him his instructions. 'I'd like a house built around two major features: a huge sunken bath and a full-sized snooker table,' George said.

It was an unusual request, and George got an unusual house. The bachelor pad was full of all the latest technology, including a button to make a TV appear out of the wall and a button to close the curtains. This was very high-tech for the 1970s!

George loved the house at first … but eventually he grew tired of it. The house got a lot of attention in the press, so his many fans knew where he lived. People visited George's house at all times of the day just to get a look at him. George hated living under that kind of spotlight. He soon sold the house and went back to Mrs Fullaway.

Charlton couldn't understand George's attitude to life – especially when it came to football. Charlton loved Manchester United, and he expected others to love it as much as he did. He certainly never approved of the lifestyle George led.

'Maybe one day they will put you in a bottle in some laboratory at Manchester University,' Charlton once said to George.

The pair had been friends on and off the pitch for a long time, and Charlton tried to show George another way of living. George was surprised when Charlton invited him to his house for dinner one night, and he was even more surprised when he said yes!

Well, who knows, I might pick up a few things from old Bobby Charlton, George thought.

George enjoyed meeting Charlton's wife and dog and seeing his home. He asked lots of questions – like how they looked after the dog and how they ran the house. It was a nice evening, and it inspired George to get a dog of his own!

But George knew that the life Charlton had wasn't for him. He was too young and too restless for a wife and kids.

That was fine with Charlton, of course. Everybody is different. But when George missed training or disappeared without telling anybody, he thought George was disrespecting the club.

'What's happening with George?' people started asking Charlton.

The manager wasn't doing anything, so Charlton stepped in and took his concerns to the club.

'It's not right for George to be treated differently from everyone else,' he said. 'It's not helping team morale at a time when we all need to pull together.'

But nothing improved.

George knew Charlton disapproved of what he was doing, but he also got annoyed with him. *He's got a holier-than-thou attitude,* George thought.

'We don't have to stick rigidly to the short back and sides and wear-your-club-blazer-at-all-times routine of the past,' George argued.

'I represent the future of Manchester United.'

But Charlton thought George could learn a thing or two from him. 'I just don't understand him,' he said to others. 'What do you come into football for? It's your duty to give your best to the people who come to support you.'

At first, no matter what was going on behind the scenes, George always gave his best on matchday. In a 1972 game against Sheffield United, he scored a goal that is still talked about today. He brought the ball under control thirty yards from the Sheffield United goal, then shifted right, beat one defender ... two defenders ... three defenders ... and blasted the ball past the diving keeper to score at the far post!

I thought I was never going to score! George thought as he celebrated.

The goal became so legendary that it was used in the opening credits for *Match of the Day*! Even Charlton reluctantly admitted that it was a terrific goal.

But George and Charlton's bad relationship off the pitch began to affect their on-the-pitch performances. At one point, they even stopped passing the ball to each other. Worse still, George refused to play in Charlton's final match before his retirement in 1973.

By then, George was considering getting out of the game himself.

'I'm sick of it,' he said. 'Right now, I'd go anywhere I thought there could be success. It's the team. It's just not good enough.'

Less than a year after Charlton retired, George also played his last game for United. The match was against Queens Park Rangers on the 1st of January 1974. In a disappointing end to George's Manchester United career, the Reds lost 3-0.

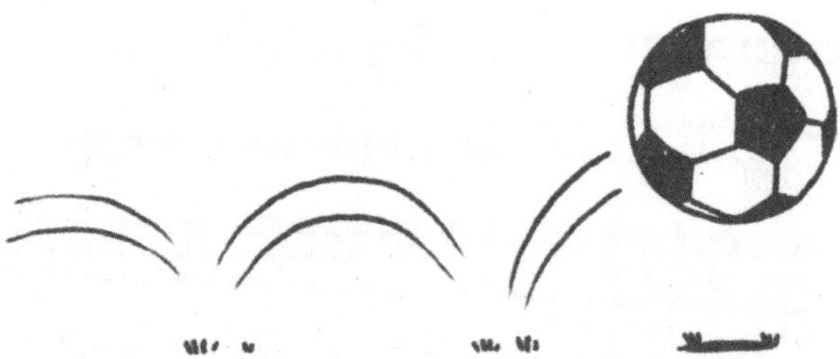

11

AN AMERICAN ADVENTURE

George played 361 league games for Manchester United and scored 136 league goals – some of which are still celebrated today. He played for lots of other clubs after he left Manchester United, but he was most excited about his time in the United States.

'I'm going to resurrect my career,' George told a friend before signing for the Los Angeles Aztecs in 1976.

This is a fresh start, thought George.

The North American Soccer League (NASL) was very different from the First Division in England back then. Football was not as popular in America as it was in the rest of the world, and not as many fans had even heard of the fabulous George Best.

Without the pressure of living up to his massive reputation, George threw himself back into his training. He started getting fitter, even playing racket ball on top of his regular football practice. The work paid off almost at once.

His coach at the Aztecs was twenty-five-year-old Terry Fisher. Fisher knew what he was dealing with and came up with a plan to get the best out of George.

'You have to first come to grips with reality,' Fisher told his squad. 'There is going to be one set of rules for George and another set for the rest of the team.'

The Aztecs won four of George's first six games. He may not have been at the peak of his form, but he was still better than most of the other players on the pitch. More importantly, George lived an anonymous life again. He didn't have to worry about being a celebrity!

One day while George was working on his car, his teammate Roy Hudson walked by. 'What are you doing?' he asked.

'Ray, I love this place. I love it,' George told him. 'I can drive around like this and nobody even looks.

Nobody even looks!'

George scored fifteen goals in twenty-one games for the Aztecs in his first season.

This blistering form and his newfound fitness meant George also got the chance to play for Northern Ireland again. His best game came in October 1976 when Northern Ireland played against the Netherlands. The Dutch had the legendary player Johan Cruyff in their team.

'So just how good is Cruyff, the man widely accepted to be the best player in the world?' asked a reporter.

'Outstanding,' said George.

'Better than you?'

'You're kidding, aren't you?' George asked. 'I tell you what I'll do tonight … I'll nutmeg Cruyff first chance I get.'

Five minutes into the game, George did exactly that. When he poked the ball through Cruyff's legs, he celebrated as if he'd scored a goal!

In George's second season in the United States, he scored eleven more goals … but he still wasn't the perfect teammate.

During one game against Toronto, George's manager warned him, 'Don't hang onto the ball so much. They'll just put numbers on you. Spread the ball around.'

George laughed. 'Seriously? Who would you rather have the ball – me or any of these guys?'

George started to get into trouble off the pitch again too, and the owners of the Aztecs eventually decided to get rid of him.

George played for various other

clubs after that, including the San Jose Earthquakes. His most memorable goal in the States came whilst he was playing for them in 1981.

The Earthquakes were 2-0 down to the Fort Lauderdale Strikers, and George had had enough.

'Give me the ball!' he screamed.

A teammate passed the ball to him. George controlled it, still thirty-five yards away from the goal. Then George showed a flash of the brilliance that never left him. He dribbled and darted past seven defenders and came face-to-face with the keeper. George didn't miss from there!

'Best … manoeuvring unbelievably!' the commentator exclaimed. 'Best still has it … I don't believe this move … That's the greatest soccer goal I've ever seen!'

It wasn't the first time somebody had said that about George Best, but it was the last. A few years later in 1984, after joining and leaving three more clubs, he made a very difficult decision and retired from football.

12

GEORGE'S LEGACY

Sadly, George died on the 25th of November 2005. He was fifty-nine years old.

When someone asked George how people would remember him after he was gone, he said, 'They'll forget all the rubbish when I've gone and they'll remember the football. If only one person thinks I'm the best player in the world that's good enough for me.'

It's fair to say that more than one person thought George was the best player in the world!

Argentinian legend Diego Maradona loved watching George as a kid. 'George inspired me when I was young,' he said. 'He was flamboyant and exciting. I think we were very similar players, dribblers who create moments of magic.'

'George was as good as anyone you will see; he used to embarrass players time and time again,' said Bobby Charlton.

Even Pelé thought George was 'the greatest footballer in the world.'

George's skills on the football field have continued to inspire generations of footballers. His 179 Manchester United goals in all competitions made him the fifth top male goalscorer at the club. To this day, his six goals against Northampton in the FA Cup are still the joint-most scored in one match for the Red Devils.

George was also the first player to make the number 7 shirt an iconic one for Manchester United. Since George's time at the club, other incredible players who have inherited the number include Eric Cantona, David Beckham and Cristiano Ronaldo. Whenever a new player dares to wear the number 7, they have a lot to live up to!

Manchester United have never forgotten George. The first game at Old Trafford after George died was against West Brom. Before the match

kicked off, the club arranged an emotional tribute. Thousands of fans laid tributes to George at a makeshift shrine outside the stadium and then observed a one-minute silence before kick-off.

Some of George's former teammates appeared on the pitch to pay their respects too. Even some of the West Brom players George played against in his 1963 debut showed up. The most heartbreaking moment came when Charlton said a few words about George.

Charlton and Law were among the people who visited George in the hospital before he passed away. Law said, 'We talked about all the stuff we did together.'

In recognition of George, Charlton and Law's achievements at the club, Manchester United paid a unique tribute to all three men via a statue. The 'Holy Trinity' statue was unveiled outside of Old Trafford in 2008, exactly forty years after George and Charlton helped the Red Devils win the European Cup in 1968.

'It really is a wonderful honour to

be alongside Sir Robert and George,' said Law, 'and I'm sure George will be looking down and admiring the statue.'

The statue is just one more way to remember George Best – a remarkable player who will forever be part of Manchester United.